Rob's New SMARTPAD

by Margaret McArthur

Illustrations by Bryan Jason Ynion (BJY)

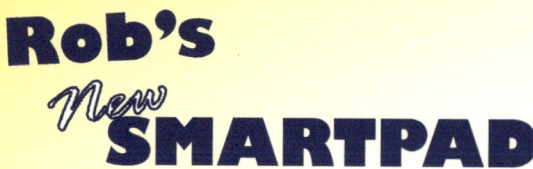

First Published by

Text copyright @ Margaret McArthur
Illustrations copyright @ Margaret McArthur

All rights reserved. No part of this publication may be used or reproduced, stored or introduced into a retrieval system, or transmitted, in any form or by any means (electronic, mechanical, photocopying, recording or otherwise), without prior written permission of the publisher - except in case of brief quotations used in reviews and/or academic articles, in which case quotations are permitted.

Written by Margaret McArthur
Illustrated by Bryan Jason Ynion (BJY)
Layout by Carolyn Tonkin Design
Printed by Ingramspark

National Library of Australia
Cataloguing-in-Publication data:
Margaret McArthur 2018

ISBN
978-0-6484449-0-9 (Paperback)
978-0-6484449-1-6 (Hardback)

For children age 6-9
Subjects covered, online presence, technology use, online grooming, personal details sharing.

First Edition

This publication contains ideas and opinions of the author and is a fictional story. It is intended as a resource for informing children on the dangers of the internet. Educators are advised to read through the book before commencing delivery to the intended audience.

The author and publisher assume no responsibility for any liability, loss or risk, personal or otherwise, which is incurred consequently, directly or indirectly, of the use and application of any content of this book.

This book is dedicated to my eldest daughter Kayleigh. Her inspiration and guidance gave me the confidence to embark on writing educational stories for young children.

Rob the Robot was celebrating his birthday.

He was playing games with his friends at his party.

When mum said, "It's time!", Rob could barely contain his **glee**.

He looked at all the gifts and gasped, **"are these all for me?"**

A scarf, some socks, and "What's that?" said Rob's dad.
In the last box was a brand new, shiny **smartpad!**

Soon, Rob downloaded lots of cool apps and games.
He gave a fake birth-date but used his real name.

A stranger befriended him, claiming to know Rob's dad.
Rob said 'Hi!', thinking his dad wouldn't get mad.

The stranger said, "I'm Tinny, and I'm twelve years old."
Rob thought he was cool, he believed all that he was told.

Tinny and Rob shared stories about fun times.
They exchanged songs they liked and upbeat rhymes.

Can you send me a selfie?

Here you go!

One day Tinny asked to see a selfie of Rob.
Rob sent it straight away, a pic of his big gob.

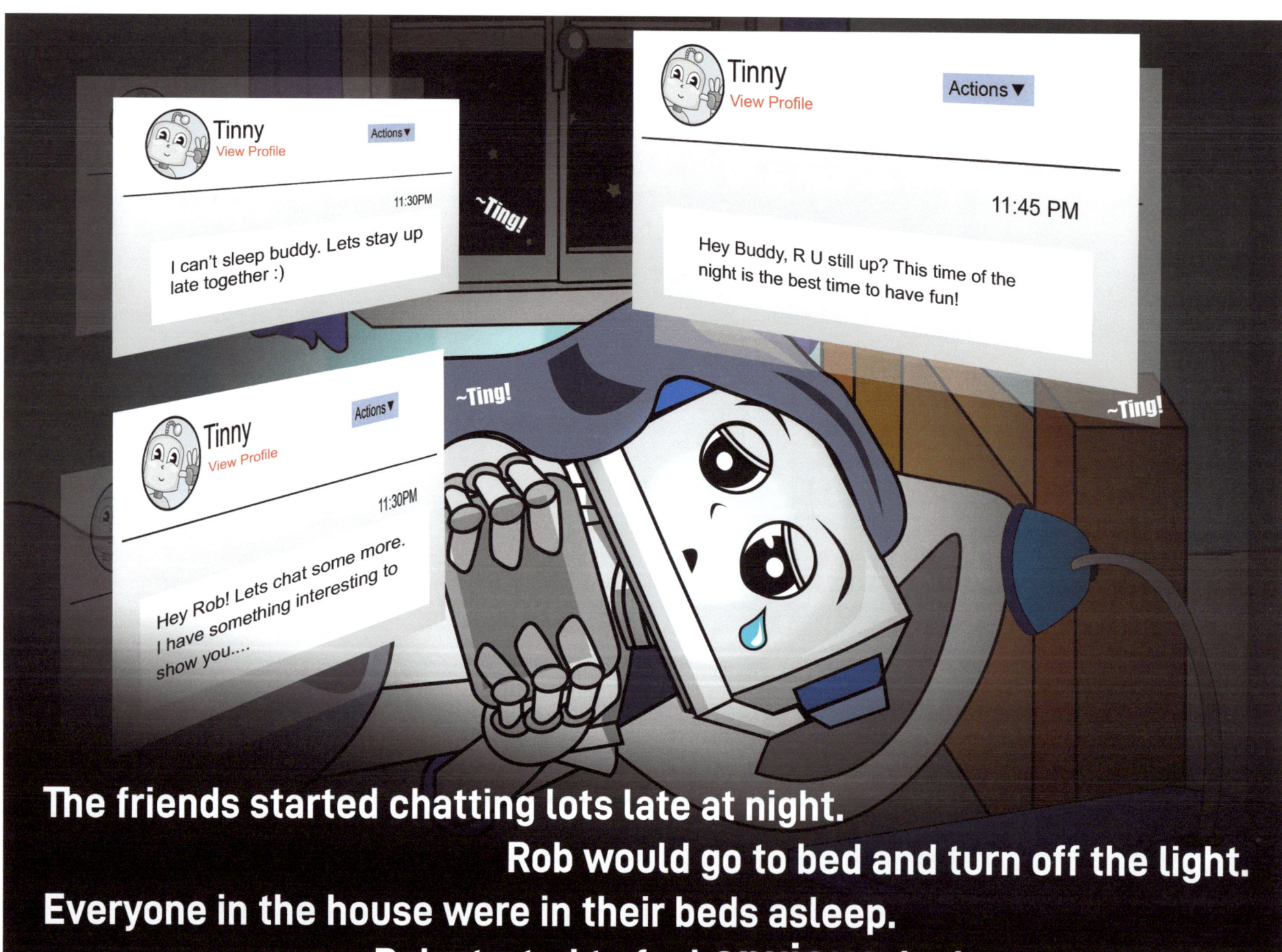

Tinny had asked for pics of parts **too bare.**

Rob began to feel troubled, but continued to share.

Tinny asked for pics of parts that were **private.**

Rob sent them, worried; he did not like it.

Tinny wasn't the same about how he chatted online. He was demanding, and requested pictures all the time.

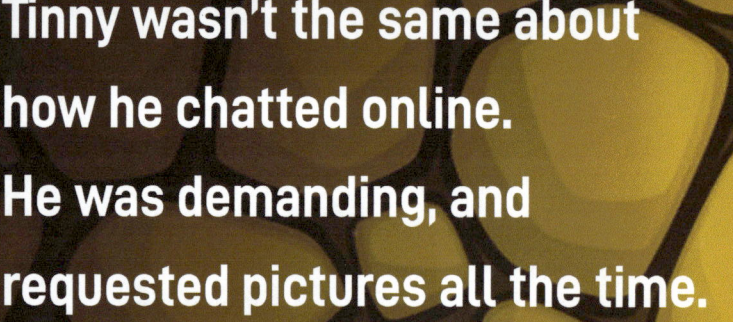

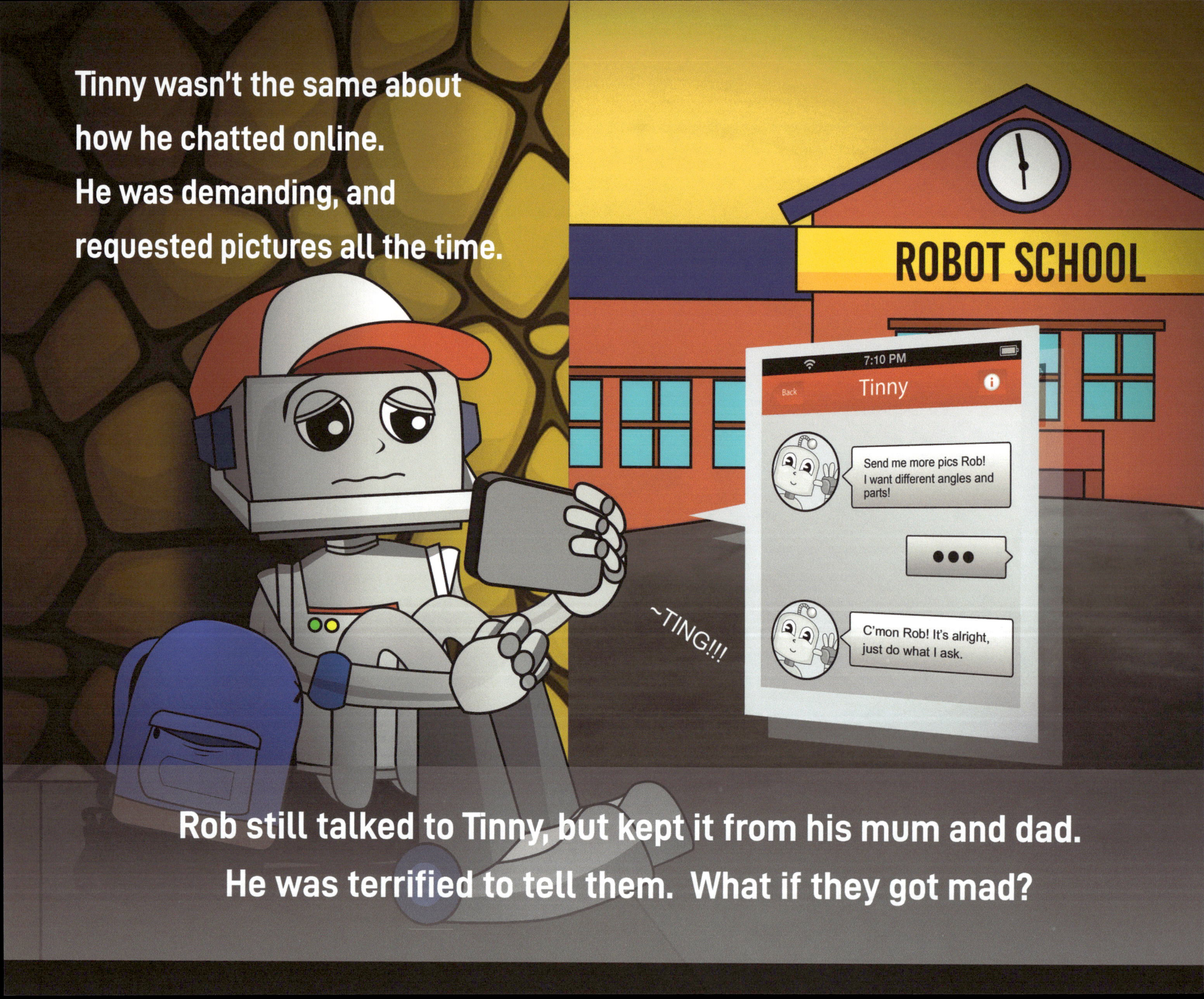

Rob still talked to Tinny, but kept it from his mum and dad. He was terrified to tell them. What if they got mad?

Then, Tinny told Rob "Meet me at the bus stop."
Rob agreed, and went to the one near the bookshop.

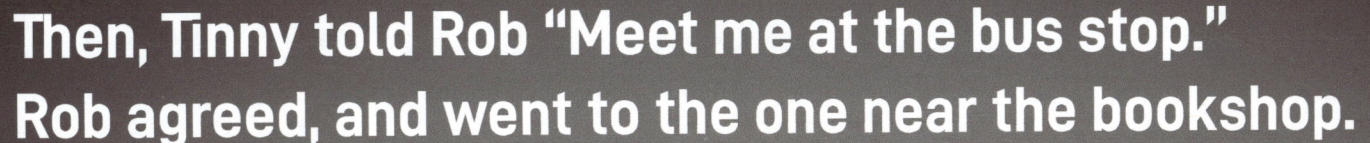

It started to get dark as the moon shone down on the street. Shadows lurked near the place they planned to meet.

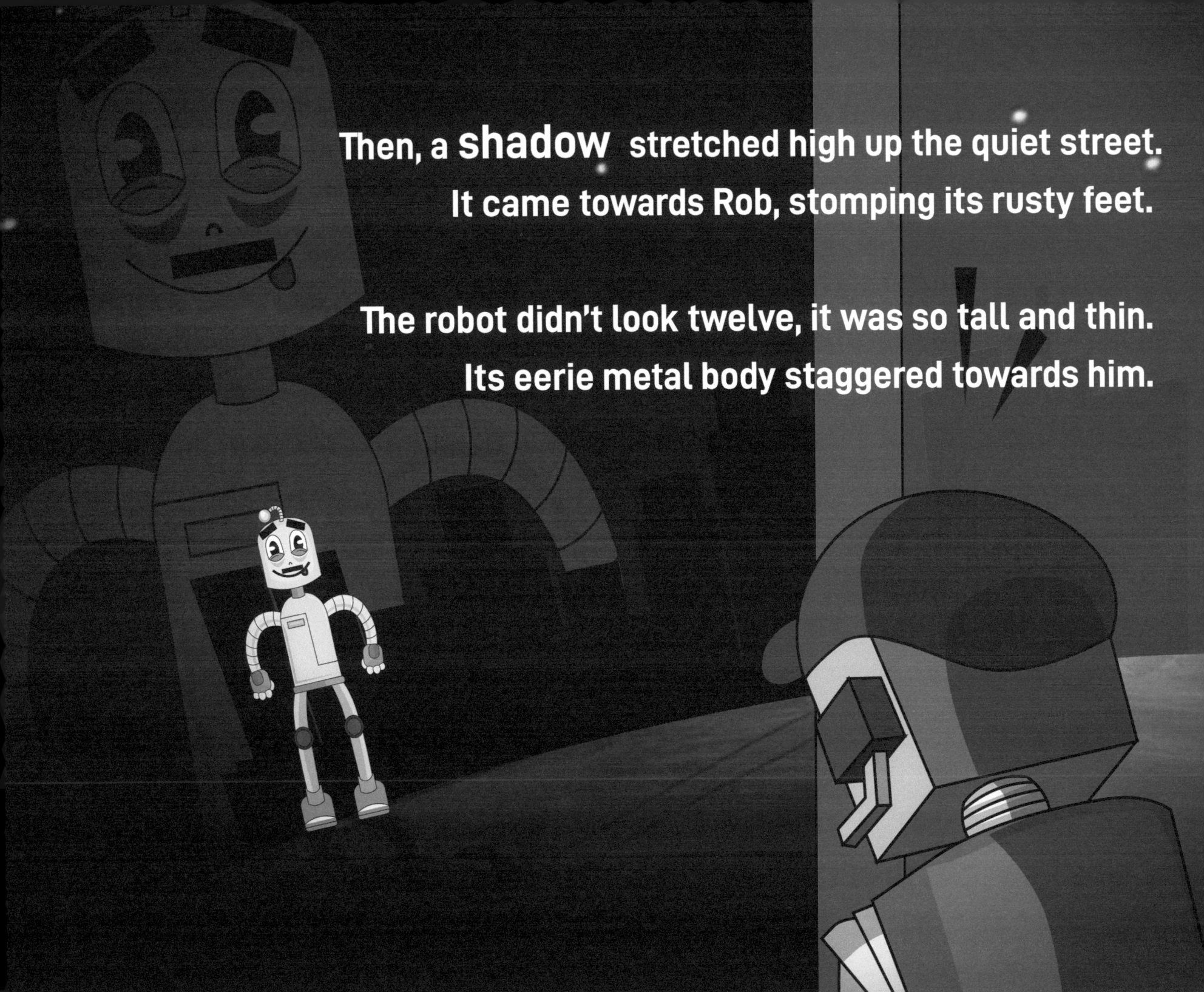

The scary robot shouted out, **"Rob, are you here?"**

Rob hid behind the lamppost, shivering with fear.

Step-by-step the robot stomped **closer**.

Rob knew he couldn't stay there any longer.

Back at home, Rob's parents realised he wasn't there.
They looked all over, but couldn't find him anywhere.
Rob's mum checked the smartpad and saw Tinny's messages.
In those chat-apps were the most troubling images.

Rob's dad had downloaded a **Find My Child** app, and with it, he found Rob not far away on the map.

Rob's parents raced to the car and drove to save Rob, but Rob didn't know this, as he hid and tried not to sob.

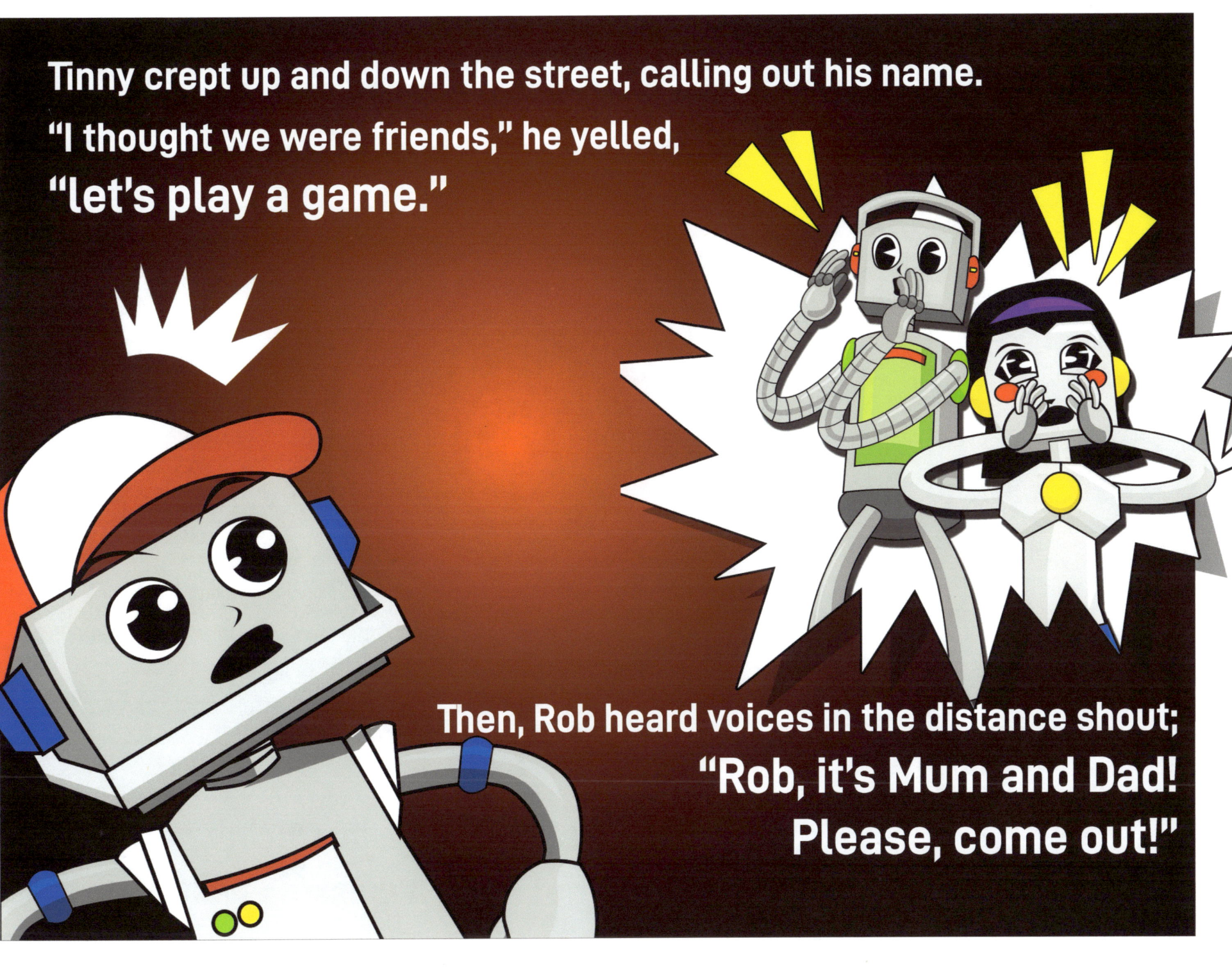

Tinny crept up and down the street, calling out his name.
"I thought we were friends," he yelled, "let's play a game."

Then, Rob heard voices in the distance shout; "Rob, it's Mum and Dad! Please, come out!"

It was a police officer who had come to arrest Tinny.

The police officer declared, "His real name is Timmy."

Rob's settings are now fixed, he's safe on the device.
His parents helped him and they all checked it twice.
They turned off some games and all the messaging apps.
It now stays out of his bedroom, even when he naps.

And now Rob knows **not to trust** what **strangers** say,

whether online, offline, at night or during the day.

Rob learned many things, including not to trust a **stranger**,

because **Timmy** was a bad bot, and with bad bots,

there is **DANGER.**

Margaret McArthur is a teacher and leader of technology in Victoria. Since starting her teaching career in Scotland over a decade ago as a Secondary Computing teacher, she discovered a passion for eLearning, which encompassed the implementation and overview of the school Cyber Awareness program. The evolution of the program required early intervention of education in the younger year levels, due to the increased use of technology at an early age. With this increase of time online, children are more exposed to the pitfalls of the internet.

With education and support, our children can learn how to make informed decisions online as they learn to keep themselves safe in the real world. This led to the creation of her cyber safe books, addressing various aspects of online dangers to protect our children from external threats.

www.margaretmcarthur.com.au

www.ingramcontent.com/pod-product-compliance
Lightning Source LLC
Chambersburg PA
CBHW041326290426

44110CB00004B/151